Complete Horoscope

Pisces 2021

Monthly astrological forecasts for 2021

TATIANA BORSCH

Translated from Russian by Sonja Swenson-Khalchenia
Translation copyright © Coinflow Limited, Cyprus
AstraArt Books is an imprint of Coinflow limited, Cyprus
Published by Coinflow Limited, Cyprus
For queries please contact: tatianaborsch@yahoo.com

ISBN: 978-9925-579-52-5 (print)
ISBN: 978-9925-579-53-2 (ebook)

Contents

2021 - Birth of a new world

Based on the events of this year, my 2020 predictions, which were published on my website and in *SWAAY* magazine, are coming true (I write this article in summer 2020). We are bearing witness to an era of change; the world is teetering on the brink, and everything we thought was permanent and unshakable has turned out not to be. What else lies ahead?

It is impossible to separate the events of 2020 and 2021. These are years of major shifts, with an effect on each country, each home, and each individual. 2020's developments will continue in 2021, and there is simply no equivalent in modern history. It's safe to say that mankind has not experienced these kinds of changes in a very long time.

Major astrological events during this period are:

The first conjunction of Saturn and Jupiter in the air element will take place in Aquarius. This extremely significant event will literally take place as 2020 becomes 2021- on December 25, 2020.

This means the dawn of the Age of Aquarius, which almost everyone has heard about.

The Age of Aquarius is very long, lasting 2,160 years. It is determined by the Earth's shift from one axis to another. This transition period from one age to another can last a long time. Many astrologers believe that it will last at least 100 years. The last 20 years have been turbulent- they were vital preparation for the adoption of new rules for a new era.

All of this means that 2020 is the last year of the outgoing Age of Pisces, and 2021 is the first year of the Age of Aquarius.

Shifting eras is always linked with global shocks, crises of civilization, and economic and cultural revolutions, as well as a new perspective on religious teachings. Even the climate usually undergoes major changes.

Summer and autumn 2020, and all of 2021, are clear indicators of that.

The second most important astrological phenomenon is conflict between Saturn and Uranus, which will continue throughout 2021.

Saturn will square Uranus several times in 2021 – we can divide them into the following periods: January-March, May-the first half of July, December 2021-January 2022.

During these periods, we can expect many problems to rear their heads. It is hard to say exactly how this will influence each individual person as part of a general prediction – everything depends on your personal data, though, generally speaking, I can say that we will see the following trends in during these periods of 2021:

I.   First of all, we can expect the economic crisis to expand in scope. Many people will lose their jobs, and companies will go bankrupt.

II. In many countries, we will see social breakdown. People will organize strikes and demonstrations, and the overarching theme will be their discontent with authorities and the current order. We will see confrontation between society and power structures.

III. In global hotspots, we may see new deployments of military force or reescalation of conflict.

IV. For individuals, problems that began in 2019 or 2020 will continue, though this time, things may worsen. Remember – a chain is only as strong as its weakest link.

V.   The climate may undergo significant changes- flooding and forest fires will cause extensive damage. Large-scale migrations will be the result. In response, governments of countries in a better position may declare states of emergency or deploy troops in order to prevent unwanted migrants from crossing their borders.

VI. This interaction between Saturn and Uranus is indicative of conflict between old and new ways of life, and a difficult, irreconcilable struggle that will be reflected in all areas of life – social, economic, and political.

Saturn carries the energy of restrictions and structure. At the same time, Uranus is the planet of unexpected, revolutionary change (as well as high tech). Conflict between the two planets leads to sharp changes in existing reality. Transitioning to a new world and a new set of rules will lead to conflict.

Interaction between Saturn and Uranus speaks to opposition to both new and old ways of living, and of the rigid, irreconcilable struggle that is reflected in every sphere of life – social, economic, and political. Most peoples' lives will undergo dramatic changes, and they will have to adapt.

Economics and Politics

Saturn will square Uranus throughout 2021, and this will raise difficult questions – it is time for out with the old, in with the new. But replacing an old system with a new one is rarely a peaceful process. That is why the struggle between old and new economic orders will be a feature of 2020 and 2021.

Former economic systems will begin to transform, right before our very eyes, and these processes will go hand in hand with trade wars, political reckoning, and in some cases, armed conflict.

As the global financial crisis further unfolds, we can expect to see a stronger China, and weakened United States. Countries in the Western financial system will suffer greatly, particularly those in the Eurozone, and American political and economic satellites.

From an astrological perspective, the American presidential elections will take place during one of the most challenging periods of 2020. By now, we are used to political scandals every four years when they occur. However, I fear that the 2020 elections will put all others to shame when it comes to political upheaval.

On Election Day and the period leading up to it, Mercury and Mars will be in retrograde, which means that there will be significant incorrect or intentionally twisted information, crowds of protesters, and this will peak the last week before the elections take place, on November 3. Retrograde planets also point toward the opposition party trying to protest the election results, which will translate into large-scale scandal.

Donald Trump may be re-elected for a second term, if Joe Biden is his only opponent. Incriminating information on Biden will come to light in late September or October 2020, when he will simultaneously battle serious health issues. Generally speaking, Biden's horoscope is much weaker than Trump's.

Whoever ends up as President of the United States will have to face a series of problems in 2021- most of all conflict among members of his inner circle.

The horoscope of the United States, which was founded on the day of its Declaration of Independence, on July 04, 1776, in Philadelphia, Pennsylvania, USA, predicts that America's economic and political might will waste away, and this may take place more quickly than we can imagine.

This crisis in the American system will lead to a drop and depreciation in the US dollar in late 2020 or the first quarter of 2021. The US chart suggests that in 2021, the dollar will be replaced as a reserve currency.

As America weakens, it will face growing confrontations with other countries. In 2021, the US will wield less influence on political and economic allies.

There may even be tides of separatism within the States themselves. Even so, I do not think the United States is threatened by the same fate as the USSR – it is unlikely to disintegrate. But it is possible that in late 2020 or early 2021, some states will declare their desire to secede, and even take some decisive steps in that direction, but full secession is not in the cards. Nonetheless, the struggle will be very difficult for America's political elite and society as a whole.

Large-scale social protests and unrest, which we saw in 2019 and 2020 will continue in 2021, though they may become more aggressive in nature.

This does not only apply to the United States. Social activism will grow worldwide. Mottos of the Age of Aquarius are FREEDOM, EQUALITY, and BROTHERHOOD, and they will be brandished in many countries around the world. This time, the conflict will not only be over ethnic or racial issues, but also pit social classes against each other – the rich versus the poor.

During the second half of 2020, and nearly all of 2021, expect an economic crisis that will spare nearly no country around the world. Many will blame their current governments, and brutal confrontations between citizens and the authorities will follow, oppositions will become active, demonstrations will take place, and instability in some countries may go so far as to topple current regimes.

England will also be dragged into financial crisis, and according to its horoscope, the worst period countrywide is likely to begin in December 2020, and last until September 2023. Expect financial problems, changes in the Royal Family (the Queen is likely to leave the throne between December 2020 and July 2021), and also innovative changes to how the country is governed.

There are also indications that in the summer and fall of 2020, a financial crisis is likely in the Russian Federation, and it will continue into 2021.

During this period, President Putin's horoscope contains indications of a systemic crisis, financial shortages, and growing opposition movements. Any leader's horoscope is largely a reflection of the state of his or her country.

Money

All countries will lean more strongly toward virtual currencies and cryptocurrencies, which will be accepted by many countries' governments over the next three to five years. This will make it easier to control cash flow, and with it, all of us.

Our reality will increasingly take place virtually, and professionals in this arena will make up the most sought-after and highly-paid class of workers.

As far as personal finance, the Zodiac sign horoscopes included in my book, "Complete Horoscope 2021" offer more specific information. But generally speaking, during a transition period, it is better to refrain from taking risks, and best to avoid investing your money in get-rich-quick schemes.

What's more, there is a saying "Don't risk your house on a sure thing"- now, that is surprisingly relevant.

Personal life

A crisis is a crisis, but love is an eternal concept. So long as humans exist, they will live and love. 2021 will likely also be a year of major changes in this arena. While tragedy will befall some, others will find happiness.

Unstable partnerships are likely to fall apart, and all the problems faced by unhappy couples are likely to rear their ugly heads.

Unexpected breakups are a possibility, and in many cases, this will be related to an existential crisis, internal discomfort, or maybe even material losses.

Couples with a sincere bond and real affection for one another may be able to take their relationship to the next level, for example, they may begin living together, or get married.

The political, economic, and social shifts underway might force many to move, find a new place to live, or acquire real estate. Many people may also find themselves immersed in issues related to housing- buying or restoring a home, and in some cases, that may be related to moving to another city or even abroad.

In that scenario, be careful and pay attention- due to the conflict between Saturn and Uranus, it is not worth making any investments in a completed construction or second home unless the project has already been proven.

People will begin to seriously reconsider their views on the concept of marriage in the near future. During the Age of Aquarius, bonds between people will be built on ideas of equality and spiritual unity.

The current trend of increasing numbers of non-traditional relationships will only grow stronger.

Differences between the sexes will gradually fade away, as Aquarius is the sign of unisex. Marriage itself will begin to resemble the classic model less and less, as it becomes free, and in some cases, "open". This may bring both advantages and serious disadvantages. Obviously, freedom is a good thing. But that freedom often goes hand in hand with loneliness.

Conflict between Saturn and Uranus will lead to a generational conflict. Saturn represents the older generation, parents, while Uranus represents rebellious children. That means that the younger generation will actively push back against pressure from their elders, and the older generation will need to become wiser and more flexible.

Health

Technology will play a greater role in medicine, affecting every branch of it.

The union of Saturn and Jupiter, and their tension toward Uranus suggest unexpected deaths, which may be due to various types of accidents and cataclysms.

Those suffering from chronic cardiovascular or spinal diseases should take special precautions.

We may encounter a "second wave" of coronavirus, or outbreaks of new, unknown diseases.

I entitled this article "Birth of a New World". Birth is a painful process, and a mother's body undergoes significant changes, but the fact remains that birth is a great joy for parents and loved ones. The same can be said for 2021. It will not be an easy year, and many will have a difficult time – whether they face problems at work or in their personal life, but that is the logical continuation of the period we live in. We will gain experience and knowledge, and see the emergence of new technology, which will open a new chapter in human history. I am certain that after a transition period, the Age of Aquarius will be the beginning of a new, wonderful world.

Tatiana Borsch

July 12, 2020

2021 Overview for Pisces

2021 will be difficult for you. You will have to adapt to circumstances that are constantly in flux, and show agility as you maneuver between the hot and cold currents surrounding you on all sides. You will not disappoint, and near the end of the year, you will be able to celebrate your victory.

Work. For most entrepreneurs and managers, 2021 will be a test of strength. Those dealing with longstanding legal problems may find themselves facing unexpected twists and turns. New claims, various audits, and visits from regulatory bodies are highly likely.

Otherwise, you may face problems with your colleagues from other cities or abroad, who may shift their intentions. The best outcome is that they throw a wrench in your joint projects, and in the worst-case scenario, they end things entirely. Alternatively, challenges on the international stage may be at fault.

Employees will face problems with coworkers, and may think about finding a better place for their talents. These opportunities are there, but not in 2021. You will have to wait until 2022.

Your first steps in negotiations on this matter are not likely to start until December 2021- keep that in mind, if you feel an urge to cut and run. Remember that in 2021, those around you will zero in on your weaknesses rather than your strengths, and therefore, keep a close eye on everything you do and say.

Critical months this year are the second half of January, February, the end of May, June, and December. By the end of December, when Jupiter enters your sign, you will be able to safely say that you have made your way to the end of the tunnel - somewhat bruised and battered, but with your head held high!

Money. Things are a bit conflicting when it comes to finances this year, though when times get tough, you can always turn to an old friend or loved one for help. They can help you with professional matters, as well as emerging financial difficulties.

Love and family. Things may be different in your personal life. Those who have been partnered up for some time will be making decisions on marriage or living together, and will certainly buy a place to live.

Pisces who quit their jobs may do so due to pregnancy or marriage.

In many families, there will be problems with relatives, though it is impossible to describe in the general forecast each particular case. There may be serious arguments, or you may find yourself involved in your close relatives' problems.

With all the problems you are facing in 2021, you will be able to count on those closest to you - your spouse or other loved ones.

Romantic Pisces and those who are sitting on the fence should keep in mind that 2021 is the year things will be brought into the light, and act accordingly.

Health. Those who are spared problems at work and at home may find themselves dealing with health issues. It is likely old chronic illnesses will exacerbate, and unexpected appearance of new issues is a strong possibility, so take care of yourself and be observant.

Throughout the year, be careful when traveling or driving - accidents and emergencies are extremely likely in 2021. If your family is expecting a child, only select medical facilities which you trust 100%!

January

You always have to fight for what you believe in, even when it seems like you have no hope of winning. In fact, you always do have a chance, and when you need it most, that chance will appear before you, plain as day.

Work. The first half of January is a great time for you to relax and combine business with pleasure, while cultivating necessary relationships at work, and having a good time. This includes meeting up with old friends, talking to your superiors, and meeting new, interesting people.

During the second half of the month, however, things will start to look dysfunctional. You will face unexpected problems, which may look different in each individual case.

Some secrets may come to light, which might damage your reputation and cast doubt on your previous achievements.

Alternatively, you may learn something about your associates and colleagues, which will force you to reconsider the relationship and lead to serious conflict.

You will also rethink relationships with colleagues from other cities or abroad. For various reasons, things will become complicated, or break off for some time.

If any of that applies to you, remember that these issues will likely not be resolved in January; they will probably become more serious next month.

Trips planned for the second half of January will likely be unsuccessful.

Money. January is likely to be a neutral month as far as your finances are concerned. Both income and expenses will be predictable and reasonable. Problems at work will not be reflected yet in your bank account, and in any case, the biggest casualty this month will be your reputation, which may affect your relationship with business partners.

Love and family. During the second half of the month, those whose interests are more focused on their personal lives will face some challenges. The first half of January will be frenetic, fun, and interesting – there may be travel, and excitement with close friends, relatives, and loved ones. However, unexpected problems may crop up during the second half of the month, requiring you to think seriously about the future of your relationships.

Secrets will come to light – either yours or those of someone close to you. Your relationship with family members will suddenly grow complicated, and you may have serious arguments. After studying the problem at hand, you will understand that you should have done something differently, that you didn't think to do in the heat of the moment. Everything will be alright, these things happen. The most important thing is to extricate yourself from the situation. Though you might fight fire with fire at work, when it comes to your personal life, this only leads to disaster. Be flexible, diplomatic, and wise – this is your trump card, and now is the time to play it.

Health. During the first half of January, you are feeling great and have no reason to fear illness.

During the second half of the month, however, you will not be so lucky. Problems may strike right in the middle of the month. This may mean that old, chronic illnesses are returning, or that new ones are appearing. During the second half of January, there is a danger of injury and emergencies. Remember that, and try to protect yourself. Drivers should be particularly careful behind the wheel- there is a high probability of traffic accidents during this period. The stars also recommend that you refrain from travel, unless it is absolutely essential. Things will not go as planned, and you will find nothing but trouble.

February

During the month of February, you will find that you are facing limits on your ability to act freely. You need to collect yourself, and take a long, hard look at the situation, before waiting it out. Don't be rash, and instead act gradually, like a courtier at the royal court.

Work. This month, a difficult situation that came up somewhat earlier, will reach its peak. Entrepreneurs and managers at every level are finding their secret enemies and competition suddenly in action, attempting to throw a wrench in the gears of anything you do.

You may face intrigue, and incorrect or deliberately misrepresented information, which will have a significant influence not only on your work, but on your reputation, as well.

Those with ties to colleagues in other cities or abroad will also face trouble. Perhaps your partners will not follow through with their responsibilities, and generally display hostility. Alternatively, *force majeure* will somehow change circumstances, making it difficult to cooperate.

Trips planned this month will be unsuccessful and bring nothing but trouble,

February is unlucky for employees, too. Expect misunderstandings with those around you, inappropriate behavior on the part of colleagues, rumors, intrigue, and gossip. During this time, old friends or someone influential may support you. This also applies to situations where old legal troubles rear their heads again, which is highly likely this month.

Things will get better closer to the end of the month, when you will be able to be more productive and active.

Money. Against this backdrop at work, financial stability is simply unrealistic. Your income is dropping, while your expenses grow, and this will continue into next month, too.

Love and family. Those who are more focused on their personal life this month will also face difficulties and challenges. Many Pisces will run into conflict with their family members. They are playing by their own rules, and you are playing by yours. It seems that you don't share the same goals, and reconciliation will not be possible this month.

Your relatives may find out something you would have preferred to keep a secret, and that information will make it difficult to smooth over the relationship. A major blowout is highly likely in mid-February, but the relationship isn't over – next month, you will be sure to find a way to reconcile.

In any case, keep your cards close, and things will be better if you remember that early on. This applies not only to spouses, but also to lovers, whose relationship is under pressure from the heavens.

Health. You are feeling incredibly lethargic this month, and those who are already weak need to be especially careful. Old, chronic ailments may return, or unexpected health issues may arise.

Young and health Pisces should also be careful, and take steps to avoid injury or accidents. Be attentive when traveling or driving. The most dangerous period for you is mid-February, from the 10th to the 14th.

March

March is very kind to you. This is a time for action, and overcoming former obstacles. Grab life by the horns, you're finally having some good luck!

Work. This month, you will cleverly avoid several problems, and those you can't avoid will require attention and careful effort on your part. However, the situation will improve significantly, and the difficult challenges you faced over the last several months are now safely resolved- if not entirely, at least in part.

When it comes to resolving the most painful issues, you can count on support from old friends or high-level mentors. Thanks to their help, you will be able to work your way out of difficult legal intrigue, and grapple with both discreet and obvious foes.

Your relationship with colleagues from other cities or abroad will be much calmer, and you might even take a successful trip or finalize negotiations. However, don't let your guard down despite the positive developments. Not everything is fully resolved, and there are still some delicate matters to deal with that you will have to deal with later.

Money. Your financial situation is rather neutral in March. You might see some improvements toward the end of the month, specifically March 24 and 25.

Love and family. You can expect some positive changes in your personal life. Chaos, confusion, and various types of intrigue will come to an end, either entirely or in part.

Thanks to your efforts, and the help of friends, your relationship with your parents will be significantly better, and, thanks to help from some friends, so is your relationship with other relatives. In any case, hostile parties will suddenly hold their tongues.

Overall, your future is looking good, and new opportunities are slowly opening their doors.

Health. This month, your well-being is looking much better, and you are quickly on the mend from any illnesses you experienced last month.

April

The changes will continue this month, and this time, they are in your favor. Look toward the future with careful optimism, and plan things out well.

Work. April may bring major changes at work, which especially concerns managers and entrepreneurs. You may see real estate transactions, profitable purchases, or profitable sales, as well. In any case, you are on the receiving end, and that is reason to celebrate.

Those with longstanding legal problems will be close to an amicable resolution. Underlying issues here have not entirely disappeared, but are improving, and any loose ends will be resolved soon.

You will still find huge support at work from old friends or some superiors, and it will be both timely and effective.

Employees will strengthen their position at work and may even receive additional income.

Your ties to colleagues from other cities or countries are slowly improving, and you might conduct peaceful negotiations, which will relieve the pressure on your relationships, and open the door to a brighter future.

Money. Your finances are noticeably improving – in addition to your usual sources of income, many Pisces might count on support from parents, loved ones, and also additional profit from various real estate transactions.

Love and family. Your personal life may turn out in many different ways, depending on each individual situation.

Spouses in a stable marriage are solving important problems related to a move, or improving your home, cottage, or other residence.

Divorcing couples will do the same, but in this case, you are dealing with dividing property, particularly your home. This time, however, things will be free of conflict, and neither side will be pushed to the point of a showdown.

Any difficult relationships with relatives will get much better. It seems that things aren't quite so bad, and you can tackle the biggest issues without an argument, tension, or fuss. Now, both sides are ready to accept their mistakes, which is the true path toward peace.

In the near future, some situations may repeat themselves, but not as severely as during the first few months of the year.

Health. This month, you are not feeling particularly energetic, but if you keep living a healthy lifestyle and taking care of yourself, you should avoid any major problems. The stars still strongly encourage you to be careful when driving, and take precautions while traveling.

May

Jupiter is a lucky planet, and it is moving into your sign, which means that things are shifting, and clearly for the better. Your life is about to change, so don't be afraid to dream – anything is possible!

Work. Many Pisces will connect their interests with colleagues from other cities or abroad, and most likely prepare for a trip. There are some bumps in the road though, which will look differently for everyone, depending on recent circumstances.

This is due to the international stage and other factors you cannot change. Be careful with documents, and check all necessary papers – this will avoid many problems, both now and down the road.

You will overcome these obstacles, assuming you make the right moves. The most persistent Pisces will be sure to do just that. Additionally, you will likely be able to count on support from friends or superiors.

Positive developments are a real possibility closer to the end of May, around that time a lot of matters will resolve in your favor.

Some Pisces will think about changing jobs, or even starting a whole new career.

Entrepreneurs might expand their areas of operations, and in various periods throughout 2021, that is sure to happen. During the second half of the month, many will look for a location to develop their business.

Money. Financially, May is likely to be neutral for you. Both your expenses and income are predictable and reasonable.

Love and family. Many Pisces might try out another lifestyle. You might make big changes in your home – repairs, buying real estate, moving to a new house, or buying a cottage.

Your relationship with family might be far from ideal, during the first half of May, and you can expect disagreements and arguments. Only through the assistance of loved ones will you be able to put these problems to rest. You may not be able to fully reconcile just yet, but you can certainly count on a fragile peace to start with.

Health. This month, you are feeling energetic and shouldn't expect to fall ill. Even so, during the first half of May, the stars strongly recommend that you take care when traveling and driving. Accidents are highly likely during this time.

June

June is a month full of contradictions. You may run into serious problems while carrying out your ideas. The stars recommend that you don't give up, don't rush things, and remember that slow and steady wins the race.

Work. When it comes to work, June is not particularly promising, especially the first twenty days of the month. This is not a favorable time for signing any contracts, or for making professional contacts with someone new.

Things are also looking gloomy when it comes to making requests to the powers that be. This is a good time, however, for meticulous administrative tasks, in order to bring everything into order.

The last ten days of June, things are looking up, but you still can't count on making any real progress at work.

During late June, many Pisces will face unexpected problems which might look very differently for everyone. There is a likelihood of unexpected run-ins with regulatory bodies, or old legal issues rearing their heads once again. Alternatively, you might deal with serious disagreements with colleagues from other cities or countries, and challenges while traveling.

You are unlikely to resolve these problems in June, and most likely, they will carry into July.

Money. Your financial outlook this month is not particularly favorable, as you can expect major expenses, and less income than usual. Most of your expenses will involve your family and home.

Love and family. For most Pisces, June will revolve around your personal life. You might expect stress related to home improvement, repairs, buying furniture, appliances, or home decoration.

The stars strongly suggest that you take your time with the most expensive purchases, and just get a good idea of everything you need until June 25. Mercury is in retrograde, so you might have to take back some of the things you bought.

In many families, once again, you are dealing with problems involving your relatives. The root of these issues began some time ago. Nothing new is expected, but old feuds will once again be resurrected.

Health. You are feeling sluggish in June, and during the middle and end of the month, you might face an unexpected force majeure. During this time, drivers and travelers need to be particularly cautious, as there is a very high likelihood of accidents.

July

Don't abandon your plans, even if you hit a wall, which you are likely to do. Keep your eye on the prize and stay the course. Be confident, but careful!

Work. During the first ten days of the month, things will be less-than ideal for you. Problems from the past will rear their heads again. In some cases, you may once again find yourself mired in legal problems, or possibly, you will face unexpected disagreements with colleagues from afar.

In other cases, this is not a problem that appeared out of thin air. You were aware of the situation, but things have taken a new and unexpected turn. Try to resolve painful issues without panicking, and keep a cool head. very soon, your troubles will be resolved, some way or another.

In addition, entrepreneurs and managers should pay close attention to their subordinates, as there may be intrigue among your team, which will carry over into the work itself.

In the case of employees, at any sign of intrigue among your colleagues, be sure to remain above the fray. You may put your foot in your mouth and see things get carried away.

Money. Your financial situation is up and down. You might be spending constantly, and in some cases, that is due to work, while in others, your personal life is the culprit. But you will not find yourself emptyhanded, and you can expect to receive the largest amounts on July 1, 2, 11, 12, 20, 21, and 28-30.

Love and family. If love or family is at the top of your priorities in life, you will have to deal with a whole host of problems this month Once again, you will face a challenging situation involving relatives, who may be ill or fall on hard times.

Alternatively, old arguments might crop up again, and this time, you can expect new information, which will simply add fuel to the fire. Someone close to you, your spouse, or children will smooth things over. One of them might reach out to hostile relatives, and facilitate the peace process.

July is favorable to couples, who might find themselves working together to overcome obstacles, and even deciding to live together.

Health. This month, you will feel much better than you have. The stars still strongly recommend being very careful while driving. The most dangerous time is the first ten days of the month, when you should also avoid any long-distance trips, as they will bring nothing but strife.

August

August will bring with it difficult tests, which, fortunately, may be the last. You can expect the seas to be less stormy soon.

Work. The first ten days of August will be the most difficult period of the month. During this time, you can expect old legal problems to rear their heads again, hostility from colleagues in other cities or abroad, and negative or deliberately mischaracterized information.

During the second half of August, and close to the end of the month, the situation may be resolved. You might see help from benevolent business partners, influential members of society, or even a friend. Their efforts will not be in vain, and in late August or September, you can expect to clear your schedule of any of the stressors bothering you now. This is also the case for those dealing with dragged out investigations. Entrepreneurs should keep an eye on their subordinates, and employees should be careful with colleagues. There is a high likelihood of conflict from August 1 to 10.

Money. Financially, August is tumultuous. You will not receive much income, but your expenses will be reasonable, too. You can expect to receive the largest sums on August 7, 8, 16, 17, and 25-27.

Love and family. You can also expect old problems to resurface in your personal life. During the first ten days of the month, many Pisces will deal with hostile relatives, and this is not the first time. Nonetheless, your spouse or loved one will help you get through this, and, in the end, things will fall into place. You will not have to wait long to find common ground with your rebellious family member.

If your loved ones are facing problems that have lasted nearly a year, the time will come when your joint efforts will lead to a favorable resolution.

Spouses' relationships will be harmonious, and the person closest to you will be a support during difficult times.

Health. Those who are happily spared personal or professional problems might see their health suffer instead. The first ten days of the month are the most dangerous time, when you are extremely likely to see old, chronic conditions return, or an unexpected appearance of new health issues. During this inauspicious period, the stars recommend that drivers and travelers take extra care – there is also a high probability of accidents and other unfortunate incidents.

September

In September, do not make any decisions until you have asked those around you for their opinion. It is better to work as part of a team – keep that in mind and don't try to make it all about you.

Work. September is a good time for meetings negotiations, and signing contracts. In all issues that have been bothering you, you are able to count on the support of associates, friends, or influential mentors. Thanks to their help, you are able to favorably resolve longstanding legal issues, handle any audits, and also establish good relations with colleagues from afar. Here, it all depends on where you are having trouble.

You will still need a few months before you are able to put a painful period at work behind you, but the main developments are happening right now.

For anything work-related, the first twenty days of September are the best time, as this is when conversations on anything that is troubling you will be extremely successful.

During the last ten days of the month, you will begin conversations on financial matters, and this will continue into October.

The first twenty days of October are a good time for those involved in the creative professions – actors, artists, and musicians. You will have the public's attention, and if you are planning a tour, it will be a smashing success.

Money. Your finances are likely to be neutral in September. You might receive support from your business partners, and it might be moral as well as financial. Those who are not part of the business world can count on help from their loved ones.

Love and family. Family issues, as well as new information about a loved one, will take up most of your energy during the first half of September. This is most relevant with regards to your relationship with relatives, which are under pressure from the heavens throughout 2021. This time, everything is different – and your spouse or someone close to you is likely to play a major role in mitigating things. Their efforts are not in vain – a conflict from someone stubborn is slowly fading away, and in the future, you will support this process. By 2022, your relationship will be calm and peaceful.

Stable couples will continue to work on home improvement projects, and, the astrologist believes, this process will move closer to a favorable ending.

September is a great time for single people, who may have unexpected encounters, an exciting romance which turns into something interesting, with a traditional ending – a marriage proposal – though the last part will have to wait until 2022.

Health. In September, you are not particularly energetic, and that will be most noticeable toward the end of the month. The astrologist believes that the best way to gain your strength is by staying busy, trying to get enough sleep, and avoiding any gossip.

October

You can expect a month full of bothersome routine, where your focus is on discipline, following schedules, and shouldering your responsibilities.

Work. October is a time for major administrative tasks, as well as various tasks related to real estate. This is also a time for work responsibilities involving red tape and financial documentation.

Be careful! Mercury will be in retrograde from September 27 to October 18, and this is usually a time rife with errors and endless re-dos.

Any disagreements with friends or former mentors are slowly working themselves out, and there is hope on the horizon that soon, they will be entirely resolved. This is relevant for anyone with longstanding legal problems, as well as those who are going through tough times with like-minded people.

Generally speaking, your overall situation is improving, and all the problems you dealt with previously are fading away. Your time will come in 2022, so hold on! That's not much longer!

Money. Financially, it's smooth sailing – but that's all you can say. For all events this month, business associates or loved ones – a spouse, parents, or elder relatives – will put funds for any basic costs.

You might also receive credit or profits from successful real estate transactions.

Love and family. Many Pisces are fully immersed in their personal lives in October. Major repair projects, new furniture and appliances, or new décor are on the agenda. Those who hadn't been able to buy a home or new apartment before might do so suddenly in October, likely in the last ten days of the month.

Any difficult relationships with relatives that vexed you in the past are slowly improving, and in the very near future, you will be a welcome guest among your unpredictable relatives.

Health. In October, you are feeling less than energetic, so take care of yourself, avoid any fall colds and infections, and avoid exacerbating any old, chronic illness.

You might tend to gain weight, so it is worth following a balanced diet.

November

November is a time for you to fight for what you believe in. Remember – victory is near! Soon, you will be beginning a new cycle in your life, and it will do away with everything that stressed you out before.

Work. During the first twenty days of November, entrepreneurs and managers will once again deal with problems from the past. In some cases, that may mean disagreements with colleagues from other cities or abroad, and in others, you will see old legal problems taking another turn.

In both cases, close to the end of the month, things will noticeably improve, and the problems will be resolved in December. In all cases, your old friends and some high-placed individuals will play an important, positive role this month. Their support will mitigate painful issues which have been bothering you for some time, and, in many cases, they will be resolved entirely.

Employees are likely to have negotiations about a new job near the need of the month, and entrepreneurs are likely to discuss a new business. In either case, things will continue on a positive track in December.

Money. In November, your finances may be up and down. Your income is not large, but your expenses are modest. Close to the end of the month, you will manage to strike a balance.

Love and family. Your personal life may take an unexpected and undesirable turn. You might have a difficult relationship with someone from your family, and this time, you can expect arguments, once again.

Your friends and someone close to you will attempt to mitigate the situation, and, thanks to their efforts, the conflict will gradually fade away, though that is only likely next month or in early 2022.

Health. This month, you are noticeably more energetic, but it's not worth testing your body's limits. Living a healthy lifestyle and being kind to yourself are still your best companions. Be attentive when traveling and driving! Accidents and unpleasant situations are highly likely, especially during the first twenty days of November.

December

The solar eclipse will take place in the highest part of your sky, and that means that December will be one of the busiest times of 2021 for you, and one of the luckiest, too.

Work. Change awaits most Pisces at work. You might get offers for a new job or start a new business, which will revive your professional life and financial outlook. Agreements reached in December might have lasting consequences, so there is good reason to pay close attention – your future is at stake!

At the same time, your previous problems are still relevant, most of all, your difficult relationship with colleagues in other cities or abroad, as well as legal matters. In either case, you can expect things to be difficult at the beginning and end of the month, but there is reason to hope that this will be the last time.

Your friends or high-level mentors might play a major role in optimizing these negative events, and their influence in all areas this month will be nothing but positive.

Money. December is a good month for you, financially. You are receiving regular income, and can expect the largest sums to come in on December 4, 5, 12, 13, 22, 23, and 31.

Love and family. In most cases, your personal life might be less exciting than work. Those who spend most of their time focused on family or romantic interests will also see longstanding problems involving close relatives resolved this month.

You might see hostilities spike again in early or late December, though this time, an old friend may serve as an intermediary. You will reach a compromise with family members, and in 2022, the situation will improve to an acceptable standard.

Issues related to your home will be resolved favorably, and many families will celebrate the holidays in a fully refurbished home or apartment.

Health. This month, you are feeling fairly energetic and are at no risk of falling ill. During the first or last ten days of the month, be careful when traveling or driving There is a very high likelihood of accidents and injuries during these periods.

A guide to Zodiac compatibility

Often, when we meet a person, we get a feeling that they are good and we take an instant liking to them. Another person, however, gives us immediate feelings of distrust, fear and hostility. Is there an astrological reason why people say that 'the first impression is the most accurate'? How can we detect those who will bring us nothing but trouble and unhappiness?

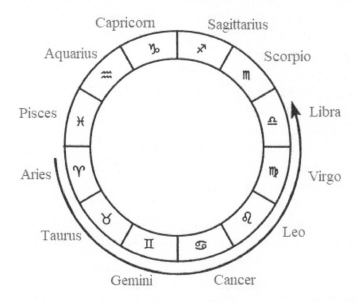

Without going too deeply into astrological subtleties unfamiliar to some readers, it is possible to determine the traits according to which friendship, love or business relationships will develop.

Let's begin with problematic relationships - our most difficult are with our **8th sign**. For example, for Aries the 8th sign is Scorpio, for Taurus it is Sagittarius and so on. Finding your 8th sign is easy; assume your own sign to be first (see above Figure) and then move eight signs counter clockwise around the Zodiac circle. This is also how the other signs (fourth, ninth and so on) that we mention are to be found.

Ancient astrologers variously referred to the 8th sign as the symbol of death, of destruction, of fated love or unfathomable attraction. In astrological terms, this pair is called 'master and slave' or 'boa constrictor and rabbit', with the role of 'master' or 'boa constrictor' being played by our 8th sign.

This relationship is especially difficult for politicians and business people.

We can take the example of a recent political confrontation in the USA. Hilary Clinton is a Scorpio while Donald Trump is a Gemini - her 8th sign. Even though many were certain that Clinton would be elected President, she lost.

To take another example, Hitler was a Taurus and his opponents – Stalin and Churchill - were both of his 8th sign, Sagittarius. The result of their confrontation is well known. Interestingly, the Russian Marshals who dealt crushing military blows to Hitler and so helped end the Third Reich - Konstantin Rokossovsky and Georgy Zhukov - were also Sagittarian, Hitler's 8th sign.

In another historical illustration, Lenin was also a Taurus. Stalin was of Lenin's 8th sign and was ultimately responsible for the downfall and possibly death of his one-time comrade-in-arms.

Business ties with those of our 8th sign are hazardous as they ultimately lead to stress and loss; both financial and moral. So, do not tangle with your 8th sign and never fight with it - your chances of winning are remote!

Such relationships are very interesting in terms of love and romance, however. We are magnetically attracted to our 8th sign and even though it may be very intense physically, it is very difficult for family life;

'Feeling bad when together, feeling worse when apart'.

As an example, let us take the famous lovers - George Sand who was Cancer and Alfred de Musset who was Sagittarius. Cancer is the 8th sign for Sagittarius, and the story of their crazy two-year love affair was the subject of much attention throughout France. Critics and writers were divided into 'Mussulist' and 'Sandist' camps; they debated fiercely about who was to blame for the sad ending to their love story - him or her. It's hard to imagine the energy needed to captivate the public for so long, but that energy was destructive for the couple. Passion raged in their hearts, but neither of them was able to comprehend their situation.

Georges Sand wrote to Musset, "*I ∎on't love you anymore, an∎ I will always a∎ore you. I ∎on't want you anymore, an∎ I can't ∎o without you. It seems that nothing but a heavenly lightning strike can heal me by ∎estroying me. Goo∎-bye! Stay or go, but ∎on't say that I am not suffering. This is the only thing that can make me suffer even more, my love, my life, my bloo∎! Go away, but kill me, leaving.*" Musset replied only in brief, but its power surpassed Sand's tirade, "*When you embrace∎ me, I felt something that is still bothering me, making it impossible for me to approach another woman.*" These two people loved each other passionately and for two years lived together in a powder keg of passion, hatred and treachery.

When someone enters into a romantic liaison with their 8th sign, there will be no peace; indeed, these relationships are very attractive to those who enjoy the edgy, the borderline and, in the Dostoevsky style, the melodramatic. The first to lose interest in the relationship is, as a rule, the 8th sign.

If, by turn of fate, our child is born under our 8th sign, they will be very different from us and, in some ways, not live up to our expectations. It may be best to let them choose their own path.

In business and political relationships, the combination with our **12th sign** is also a complicated one.

We can take two political examples. Angela Merkel is a Cancer while Donald Trump is a Gemini - her 12th sign. This is why their relations are strained and complicated and we can even perhaps assume that the American president will achieve his political goals at her expense. Boris Yeltsin (Aquarius) was the 12th sign to Mikhail Gorbachev (Pisces) and it was Yeltsin who managed to dethrone the champion of Perestroika.

Even ancient astrologers noticed that our relationships with our 12th signs can never develop evenly; it is one of the most curious and problematic combinations. They are our hidden enemies and they seem to be digging a hole for us; they ingratiate themselves with us, discover our innermost secrets. As a result, we become bewildered and make mistakes when we deal with them. Among the Roman emperors murdered by members of their entourage, there was an interesting pattern - all the murderers were the 12th sign of the murdered.

We can also see this pernicious effect in Russian history: the German princess Alexandra (Gemini) married the last Russian Tsar Nicholas II (Taurus) - he was her 12th sign and brought her a tragic death. The wicked genius Grigory Rasputin (Cancer) made friends with Tsarina Alexandra, who was his 12th sign, and was murdered as a result of their odd friendship. The weakness of Nicholas II was exposed, and his authority reduced after the death of the economic and social reformer Pyotr Stolypin, who was his 12th sign. Thus, we see a chain of people whose downfall was brought about by their 12th sign.

So, it makes sense to be cautious of your 12th sign, especially if you have business ties. Usually, these people know much more about us than we want them to and they will often reveal our secrets for personal gain if it suits them. However, the outset of these relationships is, as a rule, quite normal - sometimes the two people will be friends, but sooner or later one will betray the other one or divulge a secret; inadvertently or not.

In terms of romantic relationships, our 12th sign is gentle, they take care of us and are tender towards us. They know our weaknesses well but accept them with understanding. It is they who guide us, although sometimes almost imperceptibly. Sexual attraction is usually strong.

For example, Meghan Markle is a Leo, the 12th sign for Prince Harry, who is a Virgo. Despite Queen Elizabeth II being lukewarm about the match, Harry's love was so strong that they did marry.

If a child is our 12th sign, it later becomes clear that they know all our secrets, even those that they are not supposed to know. It is very difficult to control them as they do everything in their own way.

Relations with our **7th sign** are also interesting. They are like our opposite; they have something to learn from us while we, in turn, have something to learn from them. This combination, in business and personal relationships, can be very positive and stimulating provided that both partners are quite intelligent and have high moral standards but if not, constant misunderstandings and challenges follow. Marriage or co-operation with the 7th sign can only exist as the union of two fully-fledged individuals and in this case love, significant business achievements and social success are possible.

However, the combination can be not only interesting, but also quite complicated.

An example is Angelina Jolie, a Gemini, and Brad Pitt, a Sagittarius. This is a typical bond with a 7th sign - it's lively and interesting, but rather stressful. Although such a couple may quarrel and even part from time to time, never do they lose interest in each other.

This may be why this combination is more stable in middle-age when there is an understanding of the true nature of marriage and partnership. In global, political terms, this suggests a state of eternal tension - a cold war - for example between Yeltsin (Aquarius) and Bill Clinton (Leo).

Relations with our **9th sign** are very good; they are our teacher and advisor - one who reveals things we are unaware of and our relationships with them very often involve travel or re-location. The combination can lead to spiritual growth and can be beneficial in terms of business.

Although, for example, Trump and Putin are political opponents, they can come to an understanding and even feel a certain sympathy for each other because Putin is a Libra while Trump is a Gemini, his 9th sign.

This union is also quite harmonious for conjugal and romantic relationships.

We treat our **3rd sign** somewhat condescendingly. They are like our younger siblings; we teach them and expect them to listen attentively. Our younger brothers and sisters are more often than not born under this sign. In terms of personal and sexual relationships, the union is not very inspiring and can end quickly, although this is not always the case. In terms of business, it is fairly average as it often connects partners from different cities or countries.

We treat our **5th sign** as a child and we must take care of them accordingly. The combination is not very good for business, however, since our 5th sign triumphs over us in terms of connections and finances, and thereby gives us very little in return save for love or sympathy. However, they are very good for family and romantic relationships, especially if the 5th sign is female. If a child is born as a 5th sign to their parents, their relationship will be a mutually smooth, loving and understanding one that lasts a lifetime.

Our **10th sign** is a born leader. Depending on the spiritual level of those involved, both pleasant and tense relations are possible; the relationship is often mutually beneficial in the good times but mutually disruptive in the bad times. In family relations, our 10th sign always tries to lead and will do so according to their intelligence and upbringing.

Our **4th sign** protects our home and can act as a sponsor to strengthen our financial or moral positions. Their advice should be heeded in all cases as it can be very effective, albeit very unobtrusive. If a woman takes this role, the relationship can be long and romantic, since all the spouse's wishes are usually met one way or another. Sometimes, such couples achieve great social success; for instance, Hilary Clinton, a Scorpio is the 4th sign to Bill Clinton, a Leo. On the other hand, if the husband is the 4th sign for his wife, he tends to be henpecked. There is often a strong sexual attraction. Our 4th sign can improve our living conditions and care for us in a parental way. If a child is our 4th sign, they are close to us and support us affectionately.

Relations with our **11ᵗʰ sign** are often either friendly or patronizing; we treat them reverently, while they treat us with friendly condescension. Sometimes, these relationships develop in an 'older brother' or 'high-ranking friend' sense; indeed, older brothers and sisters are often our 11ᵗʰ sign. In terms of personal and sexual relationships, our 11ᵗʰ sign is always inclined to enslave us. This tendency is most clearly manifested in such alliances as Capricorn and Pisces or Leo and Libra. A child who is the 11ᵗʰ sign to their parents will achieve greater success than their parents, but this will only make the parents proud.

Our **2ⁿᵈ sign** should bring us financial or other benefits; we receive a lot from them in both our business and our family life. In married couples, the 2ⁿᵈ sign usually looks after the financial situation for the benefit of the family. Sexual attraction is strong.

Our **6ᵗʰ sign** is our 'slave'; we always benefit from working with them and it's very difficult for them to escape our influence. In the event of hostility, especially if they have provoked the conflict, they receive a powerful retaliatory strike. In personal relations, we can almost destroy them by making them dance to our tune. For example, if a husband doesn't allow his wife to work or there are other adverse family circumstances, she gradually becomes lost as an individual despite being surrounded by care. This is the best-case scenario; worse outcomes are possible. Our 6ᵗʰ sign has a strong sexual attraction to us because we are the fatal 8ᵗʰ sign for them; we cool down quickly, however, and often make all kinds of demands. If the relationship with our 6ᵗʰ sign is a long one, there is a danger that routine, boredom and stagnation will ultimately destroy the relationship. A child born under our 6ᵗʰ sign needs particularly careful handling as they can feel fear or embarrassment when communicating with us. Their health often needs increased attention and we should also remember that they are very different from us emotionally.

Finally, we turn to relations with **our own sign**. Scorpio with Scorpio and Cancer with Cancer get along well, but in most other cases, however, our own sign is of little interest to us as it has a similar energy. Sometimes, this relationship can develop as a rivalry, either in business or in love.

There is another interesting detail - we are often attracted to one particular sign. For example, a man's wife and mistress often have the same sign. If there is confrontation between the two, the stronger character displaces the weaker one. As an example, Prince Charles is a Scorpio, while both Princess Diana and Camilla Parker Bowles were born under the sign of Cancer. Camilla was the more assertive and became dominant.

Of course, in order to draw any definitive conclusions, we need an individually prepared horoscope, but the above always, one way or another, manifests itself.

Love description of Zodiac Signs

We know that human sexual behavior has been studied at length. Entire libraries have been written about it, with the aim of helping us understand ourselves and our partners. But is that even possible? It may not be; no matter how smart we are, when it comes to love and sex, there is always an infinite amount to learn. But we have to strive for perfection, and astrology, with its millennia of research, twelve astrological types, and twelve zodiac signs, may hold the key. Below, you will find a brief and accurate description of each zodiac sign's characteristics in love, for both men and women.

Men

ARIES

Aries men are not particularly deep or wise, but they make up for it in sincerity and loyalty. They are active, even aggressive lovers, but a hopeless romantic may be lurking just below the surface. Aries are often monogamous and chivalrous men, for whom there is only one woman (of course, in her absence, they can sleep around with no remorse). If the object of your affection is an Aries, be sure to give him a lot of sex, and remember that for an Aries, when it comes to sex, anything goes. Aries cannot stand women who are negative or disheveled. They need someone energetic, lively, and to feel exciting feelings of romance.

The best partner for an Aries is Cancer, Sagittarius, or Leo. Aquarius can also be a good match, but the relationship will be rather friendly in nature. Partnering with a Scorpio or Taurus will be difficult, but they can be stimulating lovers for an Aries. Virgos are good business contacts, but a poor match as lovers or spouses.

TAURUS

A typical Taurean man is warm, friendly, gentle, and passionate, even if he doesn't always show it. He is utterly captivated by the beauty of the female body, and can find inspiration in any woman. A Taurus has such excess physical and sexual prowess, that to him, sex is a way to relax and calm down. He is the most passionate and emotional lover of the Zodiac, but he expects his partner to take the initiative, and if she doesn't, he will easily find someone else. Taureans rarely divorce, and are true to the end – if not sexually, at least spiritually. They are secretive, keep their cards close, and may have secret lovers. If a Taurus does not feel a deep emotional connection with someone, he won't be shy to ask her friends for their number. He prefers a voluptuous figure over an athletic or skinny woman.

The best partners for a Taurus are Cancer, Virgo, Pisces, or Scorpio. Sagittarius can show a Taurus real delights in both body and spirit, but they are unlikely to make it down the aisle. They can have an interesting relationship with an Aquarius – these signs are very different, but sometimes can spend their lives together. They might initially feel attracted to an Aries, before rejecting her.

GEMINI

The typical Gemini man is easygoing and polite. He is calm, collected, and analytical. For a Gemini, passion is closely linked to intellect, to the point that they will try to find an explanation for their actions before carrying them out. But passion cannot be explained, which scares a Gemini, and they begin jumping from one extreme to the other. This is why you will find more bigamists among Geminis than any other sign of the Zodiac. Sometimes, Gemini men even have two families, or divorce and marry several times throughout the course of their lives. This may be because they simply can't let new and interesting experiences pass them by. A Gemini's wife or lover needs to be smart, quick, and always looking ahead. If she isn't, he will find a new object for his affection.

Aquarians, Libras, and Aries make good partners for a Gemini. A Sagittarius can be fascinating for him, but they will not marry before he reaches middle age, as both partners will be fickle while they are younger. A Gemini and Scorpio are likely to be a difficult match, and the Gemini will try to wriggle out of the Scorpio's tight embrace. A Taurus will be an exciting sex partner, but their partnership won't be for long, and the Taurus is often at fault.

CANCER

Cancers tend to be deep, emotional individuals, who are both sensitive and highly sexual. Their charm is almost mystical, and they know how to use it. Cancers may be the most promiscuous sign of the Zodiac, and open to absolutely anything in bed. Younger Cancers look for women who are more mature, as they are skilled lovers. As they age, they look for someone young enough to be their own daughter, and delight in taking on the role of a teacher. Cancers are devoted to building a family and an inviting home, but once they achieve that goal, they are likely to have a wandering eye. They will not seek moral justification, as they sincerely believe it is simply something everyone does. Their charm works in such a way that women are deeply convinced they are the most important love in a Cancer's life, and that circumstances are the only thing preventing them from being together. Remember that a Cancer man is a master manipulator, and will not be yours unless he is sure you have throngs of admirers. He loves feminine curves, and is turned on by exquisite fragrances. Cancers don't end things with old lovers, and often go back for a visit after a breakup. Another type of Cancer is rarer – a faithful friend, and up for anything in order to provide for his wife and children. He is patriotic and a responsible worker.

Scorpios, Pisces, and other Cancers are a good match. A Taurus can make for a lasting relationship, as both signs place great value on family and are able to get along with one another. A Sagittarius will result in fights and blowouts from the very beginning, followed by conflicts and breakups. The Sagittarius will suffer the most. Marriage to an Aries isn't off the table, but it won't last very long.

LEO

A typical Leo is handsome, proud, and vain, with a need to be the center of attention at all times. They often pretend to be virtuous, until they are able to actually master it. They crave flattery, and prefer women who comply and cater to them. Leos demand unconditional obedience, and constant approval. When a Leo is in love, he is fairly sexual, and capable of being devoted and faithful. Cheap love affairs are not his thing, and Leos are highly aware of how expensive it is to divorce. They make excellent fathers. A Leo's partner needs to look polished and well-dressed, and he will not tolerate either frumpiness or nerds.

Aries, Sagittarius, and Gemini make for good matches. Leos are often very beguiling to Libras; this is the most infamous astrological "master-slave" pairing. Leos are also inexplicably drawn to Pisces – this is the only sign capable of taming them. A Leo and Virgo will face a host of problems sooner or later, and they might be material in nature. The Virgo will attempt to conquer him, and if she does, a breakup is inevitable.

VIRGO

Virgo is a highly intellectual sign, who likes to take a step back and spend his time studying the big picture. But love inherently does not lend itself to analysis, and this can leave Virgos feeling perplexed. While Virgo is taking his time, studying the object of his affection, someone else will swoop in and take her away, leaving him bitterly disappointed. Perhaps for that reason, Virgos tend to marry late, but once they are married, they remain true, and hardly ever initiate divorce. In bed, they are modest and reserved, as they see sex as some sort of quirk of nature, designed solely for procreation. Most Virgos have a gifted sense of taste, hearing, and smell. They cannot tolerate pungent odors and can be squeamish; they believe their partners should always take pains to be very clean. Virgos usually hate over-the-top expressions of love, and are immune to sex as a mean s of control. Many Virgos are stingy and more appropriate as husbands than lovers. Male Virgos tend to be monogamous, though if they are unhappy or disappointed with their partner, they may begin to look for comfort elsewhere and often give in to drunkenness.

Taurus, Capricorn, and Scorpio make the best partners for a Virgo. They may feel inexplicable attraction for Aquarians. They will form friendships with Aries, but rarely will this couple make it down the aisle. With Leos, be careful – this sign is best as a lover, not a spouse.

LIBRA

Libra is a very complex, wishy-washy sign. They are constantly seeking perfection, which often leaves them in discord with the reality around them. Libra men are elegant and refined, and expect no less from their partner. Many Libras treat their partners like a beautiful work of art, and have trouble holding onto the object of their affection. They view love itself as a very abstract concept, and can get tired of the physical aspect of their relationship. They are much more drawn to intrigue and the chase- dreams, candlelit evenings, and other symbols of romance. A high percentage of Libra men are gay, and they view sex with other men as the more elite option. Even when Libras are unhappy in their marriages, they never divorce willingly. Their wives might leave them, however, or they might be taken away by a more decisive partner.

Aquarius and Gemini make the best matches for Libras. Libra can also easily control an independent Sagittarius, and can easily fall under the influence of a powerful and determined Leo, before putting all his strength and effort into breaking free. Relationships with Scorpios are difficult; they may become lovers, but will rarely marry.

SCORPIO

Though it is common to perceive Scorpios as incredibly sexual, they are, in fact, very unassuming, and never brag about their exploits. They will, however, be faithful and devoted to the right woman. The Scorpio man is taciturn, and you can't expect any tender words from him, but he will defend those he loves to the very end. Despite his outward control, Scorpio is very emotional; he needs and craves love, and is willing to fight for it. Scorpios are incredible lovers, and rather than leaving them tired, sex leaves them feeling energized. They are always sexy, even if they aren't particularly handsome. They are unconcerned with the ceremony of wooing you, and more focused on the act of love itself.

Expressive Cancers and gentle, amenable Pisces make the best partners. A Scorpio might also fall under the spell of a Virgo, who is adept at taking the lead. Sparks might fly between two Scorpios, or with a Taurus, who is perfect for a Scorpio in bed. Relationships with Libras, Sagittarians, and Aries are difficult.

SAGITTARIUS

Sagittarian men are lucky, curious, and gregarious. Younger Sagittarians are romantic, passionate, and burning with desire to experience every type of love. Sagittarius is a very idealistic sign, and in that search for perfection, they tend to flit from one partner to another, eventually forgetting what they were even looking for in the first place. A negative Sagittarius might have two or three relationships going on at once, assigning each partner a different day of the week. On the other hand, a positive Sagittarius will channel his powerful sexual energy into creativity, and take his career to new heights. Generally speaking, after multiple relationships and divorces, the Sagittarian man will conclude that his ideal marriage is one where his partner is willing to look the other way.

Aries and Leo make the best matches for a Sagittarius. He might fall under the spell of a Cancer, but would not be happy being married to her. Gemini can be very intriguing, but will only make for a happy marriage after middle age, when both partners are older and wiser.

Younger Sagittarians often marry Aquarian women, but things quickly fall apart. Scorpios can make for an interesting relationship, but if the Sagittarius fails to comply, divorce is inevitable.

CAPRICORN

Practical, reserved Capricorn is one of the least sexual signs of the Zodiac. He views sex as an idle way to pass the time, and something he can live without, until he wants to start a family. He tends to marry late, and almost never divorces. Young Capricorns are prone to suppressing their sexual desires, and only discover them later in life, when they have already achieved everything a real man needs – a career and money. We'll be frank – Capricorn is not the best lover, but he can compensate by being caring, attentive, and showering you with valuable gifts. Ever cautious, Capricorn loves to schedule his sexual relationships, and this is something partners will just have to accept. Women should understand that Capricorn needs some help relaxing – perhaps with alcohol. They prefer inconspicuous, unassuming women, and run away from a fashion plate.

The best partners for a Capricorn are Virgo, Taurus, or Scorpio. Cancers might catch his attention, and if they marry, it is likely to be for life. Capricorn is able to easily dominate Pisces, and Pisces-Capricorn is a well-known "slave and master" combination. Relationships with Leos tend to be erratic, and they are unlikely to wed. Aries might make for a cozy family at first, but things will cool off quickly, and often, the marriage only lasts as long as Capricorn is unwilling to make a change in his life.

AQUARIUS

Aquarian men are mercurial, and often come off as peculiar, unusual, or aloof, and detached. Aquarians are turned on by anything novel or strange, and they are constantly looking for new and interesting people. They are stimulated by having a variety of sexual partners, but they consider this to simply be normal life, rather than sexually immoral. Aquarians are unique – they are more abstract than realistic, and can be cold and incomprehensible, even in close relationships. Once an Aquarius gets married, he will try to remain within the realm of decency, but often fails. An Aquarian's partners need uncommon patience, as nothing they do can restrain him. Occasionally, one might encounter another kind of Aquarius – a responsible, hard worker, and exemplary family man.

The best matches for an Aquarius are female fellow Aquarians, Libras, and Sagittarians. When Aquarius seeks out yet another affair, he is not choosy, and will be happy with anyone.

PISCES

Pisces is the most eccentric sign of the Zodiac. This is reflected in his romantic tendencies and sex life. Pisces men become very dependent on those with whom they have a close relationship. Paradoxically, they are simultaneously crafty and childlike when it comes to playing games, and they are easily deceived. As a double bodied sign, Pisces rarely marry just once, as they are very sexual, easily fall in love, and are constantly seeking their ideal. Pisces are very warm people, who love to take care of others and are inclined toward "slave-master" relationships, in which they are the submissive partner. But after catering to so many lovers, Pisces will remain elusive. They are impossible to figure out ahead of time – today, they might be declaring their love for you, but tomorrow, they may disappear – possibly forever! To a Pisces, love is a fantasy, illusion, and dream, and they might spend their whole lives in pursuit of it. Pisces who are unhappy in love are vulnerable to alcoholism or drug addiction.

Cancer and Scorpio make the best partners for a Pisces. He is also easily dominated by Capricorn and Libra, but in turn will conquer even a queen-like Leo. Often, they are fascinated by Geminis – if they marry, it will last a long time, but likely not forever. Relationships with Aries and Sagittarians are erratic, though initially, things can seem almost perfect.

Women

ARIES

Aries women are leaders. They are decisive, bold, and very protective. An Aries can take initiative and is not afraid to make the first move. Her ideal man is strong, and someone she can admire. But remember, at the slightest whiff of weakness, she will knock him off his pedestal. She does not like dull, whiny men, and thinks that there is always a way out of any situation. If she loves someone, she will be faithful. Aries women are too honest to try leading a double life. They are possessive, jealous, and not only will they not forgive those who are unfaithful, their revenge may be brutal; they know no limits. If you can handle an Aries, don't try to put her in a cage; it is best to give her a long leash. Periodically give her some space – then she will seek you out herself. She is sexual, and believe that anything goes in bed.

Her best partners are a Sagittarius or Leo. A Libra can make a good match after middle age, once both partners have grown wiser and settled down a bit. Gemini and Aquarius are only good partners during the initial phase, when everything is still new, but soon enough, they will lose interest in each other. Scorpios are good matches in bed, but only suitable as lovers.

TAURUS

Taurean women possess qualities that men often dream about, but rarely find in the flesh – they are soft, charming, practical, and reliable – they are very caring and will support their partner in every way. A Taurus is highly sexual, affectionate, and can show a man how to take pleasure to new heights. She is also strong and intense. If she is in love, she will be faithful. But when love fades away, she might find someone else on the side, though she will still fight to save her marriage, particularly if her husband earns good money. A Taurus will not tolerate a man who is disheveled or disorganized, and anyone dating her needs to always be on his toes. She will expect gifts, and likes being taken to expensive restaurants, concerts, and other events. If you argue, try to make the first peace offering, because a Taurus finds it very hard to do so – she might withdraw and ruminate for a long time. Never air your dirty laundry; solve all your problems one-on-one.

Scorpio, Virgo, Capricorn, and Cancer make the best matches. A relationship with an Aries or Sagittarius would be difficult. There is little attraction between a Taurus and a Leo, and initially Libras can make for a good partner in bed, but things will quickly cool off and fall apart. A Taurus and Aquarius make an interesting match – despite the difference in signs, their relationships are often lasting, and almost lifelong.

GEMINI

Gemini women are social butterflies, outgoing, and they easily make friends, and then break off the friendship, if people do not hold their interest. A Gemini falls in love hard, is very creative, and often fantasizes about the object of her affection. She is uninterested in sex without any attachment, loves to flirt, and, for the most part, is not particularly affectionate. She dreams of a partner who is her friend, lover, and a romantic, all at once. A Gemini has no use for a man who brings nothing to the table intellectually. That is a tall order, so Geminis often divorce and marry several times. Others simply marry later in life. Once you have begun a life together, do not try to keep her inside – she needs to travel, explore, socialize, attend events and go to the theater. She cannot tolerate possessive men, so avoid giving her the third degree, and remember that despite her flirtatious and social nature, she is, in fact, faithful – as long as you keep her interested and she is in love. Astrologists believe that Geminis do not know what they need until age 29 or 30, so it is best to hold off on marriage until then.

Leo and Libra make the best matches. A relationship with a Cancer is likely, though complex, and depends solely on the Cancer's affection. A Gemini and Sagittarius can have an interesting, dynamic relationship, but these are two restless signs, which might only manage to get together after ages 40-45, once they have had enough thrills out of life and learned to be patient. Relationships with a Capricorn are very difficult, and almost never happen. The honeymoon stage can be wonderful with a Scorpio, but each partner will eventually go their own way, before ending things. A Gemini and Pisces union can also be very interesting – they are drawn to each other, and can have a wonderful relationship, but after a while, the cracks start to show and things will fall apart. An Aquarius is also not a bad match, but they will have little sexual chemistry.

CANCER

Cancers can be divided into two opposing groups. The first includes a sweet and gentle creature who is willing to dedicate her life to her husband and children. She is endlessly devoted to her husband, especially if he makes a decent living and remains faithful. She views all men as potential husbands, which means it is dangerous to strike up a relationship with her if your intentions are not serious; she can be anxious and clingy, sensitive and prone to crying. It is better to break things to her gently, rather than directly spitting out the cold, hard truth. She wants a man who can be a provider, though she often earns well herself. She puts money away for a rainy day, and knows how to be thrifty, for the sake of others around her, rather than only for herself. She is an excellent cook and capable of building an inviting home for her loved ones. She is enthusiastic in bed, a wonderful wife, and a caring mother.

The second type of Cancer is neurotic, and capable of creating a living hell for those around her. She believes that the world is her enemy, and manages to constantly find new intrigue and machinations.

Another Cancer, Virgo, Taurus, Scorpio, and Pisces make the best matches. A Cancer can often fall in love with a Gemini, but eventually, things will grow complicated, as she will be exhausted by a Gemini's constant mood swings and cheating. A Cancer and Sagittarius will initially have passionate sex, but things will quickly cool off. A relationship with a Capricorn is a real possibility, but only later in life, as while they are young, they are likely to fight and argue constantly. Cancer can also have a relationship with an Aries, but this will not be easy.

LEO

Leos are usually beautiful or charming, and outwardly sexual. And yet, appearances can be deceiving – they are not actually that interested in sex. Leo women want to be the center of attention and men running after them boosts their self-esteem, but they are more interested in their career, creating something new, and success than sex. They often have high-powered careers and are proud of their own achievements. Their partners need to be strong; if a Leo feels a man is weak, she can carry him herself for a while- before leaving him. It is difficult for her to find a partner for life, as chivalrous knights are a dying breed, and she is not willing to compromise. If you are interested in a Leo, take the initiative, admire her, and remember that even a queen is still a woman. Timid men or tightwads need not apply. Leos like to help others, but they don't need a walking disaster in their life. If they are married and in love, they are usually faithful, and petty gossip isn't their thing. Leo women make excellent mothers, and are ready to give their lives to their children. Their negative traits include vanity and a willingness to lie, in order to make themselves look better.

Sagittarius, Aries, and Libra make the best matches. Leos can also have an interesting relationship with a Virgo, though both partners will weaken each other. Life with a Taurus will lead to endless arguments – both signs are very stubborn, and unwilling to give in. Leos and Pisces are another difficult pair, as she will have to learn to be submissive if she wants to keep him around. A relationship with a Capricorn will work if there is a common denominator, but they will have little sexual chemistry. Life with a Scorpio will be turbulent to say the least, and they will usually break up later in life.

VIRGO

Virgo women are practical, clever, and often duplicitous. Marrying one isn't for everyone. She is a neat freak to the point of annoying those around her. She is also an excellent cook, and strives to ensure her children receive the very best by teaching them everything, and preparing them for a bright future. She is also thrifty – she won't throw money around, and, in fact, won't even give it to her husband. She has no time for rude, macho strongmen, and is suspicious of spendthrifts. She will not be offended if you take her to a cozy and modest café rather than an elegant restaurant. Virgos are masters of intrigue, and manage to outperform every other sign of the Zodiac in this regard. Virgos love to criticize everyone and everything; to listen to them, the entire world is simply a disaster and wrong, and only she is the exception to this rule. Virgos are not believed to be particularly sexual, but there are different variations when it comes to this. Rarely, one finds an open-minded Virgo willing to try anything, and who does it all on a grand scale – but she is rather the exception to this general rule.

The best matches for a Virgo are Cancer, Taurus, and Capricorn. She also can get along well with a Scorpio, but will find conflict with Sagittarius. A Pisces will strike her interest, but they will rarely make it down the aisle. She is often attracted to an Aquarius, but they would drive each other up the wall were they to actually marry. An Aries forces Virgo to see another side of life, but here, she will have to learn to conform and adapt.

LIBRA

Female Libras tend to be beautiful, glamorous, or very charming. They are practical, tactical, rational, though they are adept at hiding these qualities behind their romantic and elegant appearance. Libras are drawn to marriage, and are good at imagining the kind of partner they need. They seek out strong, well-off men and are often more interested in someone's social status and bank account than feelings. The object of their affection needs to be dashing, and have a good reputation in society. Libras love expensive things, jewelry, and finery. If they are feeling down, a beautiful gift will instantly cheer them up. They will not tolerate scandal or conflict, and will spend all their energy trying to keep the peace, or at least the appearance thereof. They do not like to air their dirty laundry, and will only divorce in extreme circumstances. They are always convinced they are right and react to any objections as though they have been insulted. Most Libras are not particularly sexual, except those with Venus or the Moon in Scorpio.

Leos, Geminis, and Aquarians make good matches. Libra women are highly attracted to Aries men - this is a real case of opposites attract. They can get along with a Sagittarius, though he will find that Libras are too proper and calm. Capricorn, Pisces, and Cancer are all difficult matches. Things will begin tumultuously with a Taurus, before each partner goes his or her own way.

SCORPIO

Scorpio women may appear outwardly restrained, but there is much more bubbling below the surface. They are ambitious with high self-esteem, but often wear a mask of unpretentiousness. They are the true power behind the scenes, the one who holds the family together, but never talk about it. Scorpios are strong-willed, resilient, and natural survivors. Often, Scorpios are brutally honest, and expect the same out of those around them. They do not like having to conform, and attempt to get others to adapt to them, as they honestly believe everyone will be better off that way. They are incredibly intuitive, and not easily deceived. They have an excellent memory, and can quickly figure out which of your buttons to push. They are passionate in bed, and their temperament will not diminish with age. When she is sexually frustrated, a Scorpio will throw all of her energy into her career or her loved ones. She is proud, categorical, and "if you don't do it right, don't do it at all" is her motto. Scorpio cannot be fooled, and she will not forgive any cheating. Will she cheat herself? Yes! But it will not break up her family, and she will attempt to keep it a secret. Scorpios are usually attractive to men, even if they are not particularly beautiful. They keep a low profile, though they always figure out their partner, and give them some invisible sign. There is also another, selfish type of Scorpio, who will use others for as long as they need them, before unceremoniously casting them aside.

Taurus is a good match; they will have excellent sexual chemistry and understand each other. Scorpio and Gemini are drawn to each other, but are unlikely to stay together long enough to actually get married. Cancer can be a good partner as well, but Cancers are possessive, while Scorpios do not like others meddling in their affairs, though they can later resolve their arguments in bed. Scorpio and Leo are often found together, but their relationship can also be very complicated. Leos are animated and chipper, while Scorpios, who are much deeper and more stubborn, see Leos as not particularly serious or reliable. One good example of this is Bill (a Leo) and Hillary (a Scorpio) Clinton. Virgo can also make a good partner, but when Scorpio seemingly lacks emotions, he will look for them elsewhere. Relationships with Lira are strange and very rare. Scorpio sees Libra as too insecure, and Libra does not appreciate Scorpio's rigidity. Two Scorpios together make an excellent marriage! Sagittarius and Scorpio are unlikely to get together, as she will think he is shallow and rude. If they do manage to get married, Scorpio's drive and persistence is the only thing that will make the marriage last. Capricorn is also not a bad match, and while Scorpio finds Aquarius attractive, they will rarely get married, as they are simply speaking different languages! Things are alright with a Pisces, as both signs are emotional, and Pisces can let Scorpio take the lead when necessary.

SAGITTARIUS

Sagittarius women are usually charming, bubbly, energetic, and have the gift of gab. They are kind, sincere, and love people. They are also straightforward, fair, and very ambitious, occasionally to the point of irritating those around them. But telling them something is easier than not telling them, and they often manage to win over their enemies. Sagittarius tends to have excellent intuition, and she loves to both learn and teach others. She is a natural leader, and loves taking charge at work and at home. Many Sagittarian women have itchy feet, and prefer all kinds of travel to sitting at home. They are not particularly good housewives – to be frank, cooking and cleaning is simply not for them. Their loved ones must learn to adapt to them, but Sagittarians themselves hate any pressure. They are not easy for men to handle, as Sagittarians want to be in charge. Sagittarius falls in love easily, is very sexual and temperamental, and may marry multiple times. Despite outward appearances, Sagittarius is a very lonely sign. Even after she is married with children, she may continue living as if she were alone; you might say she marches to the beat of her own drum. Younger

Sagittarians can be reckless, but as they mature, they can be drawn to religion, philosophy, and the occult.

Aries and Leo make the best matches, as Sagittarius is able to bend to Leo's ways, or at least pretend to. Sagittarians often end up with Aquarians, but their marriages do not tend to be for the long haul. They are attracted to Geminis, but are unlikely to marry one until middle age, when both signs have settled down. Sagittarius and Cancer have incredible sexual chemistry, but an actual relationship between them would be tumultuous and difficult. Capricorn can make a good partner- as long as they are able to respect each other's quirks. Sagittarius rarely ends up with a Virgo, and while she may often meet Pisces, things are unlikely to go very far.

CAPRICORN

Capricorn women are conscientious, reliable, organized, and hard-working. Many believe that life means nothing but work, and live accordingly. They are practical, and not particularly drawn to parties or loud groups of people. But if someone useful will be there, they are sure to make an appearance. Capricorn women are stingy, but not as much as their male counterparts. They are critical of others, but think highly of themselves. Generally, they take a difficult path in life, but thanks to their dedication, perseverance, and willingness to push their own limits, they are able to forge their own path, and by 45 or 50, they can provide themselves with anything they could want. Capricorn women have the peculiarity of looking older than their peers when they are young, and younger than everyone else once they have matured. They are not particularly sexual, and tend to be faithful partners. They rarely divorce, and even will fight until the end, even for a failed marriage. Many Capricorns have a pessimistic outlook of life, and have a tendency to be depressed. They are rarely at the center of any social circle, but are excellent organizers. They have a very rigid view of life and love, and are not interested in a fling, as marriage is the end goal. As a wife, Capricorn is simultaneously difficult and reliable. She is difficult because of her strict nature and difficulty adapting. But she will also take on all the household duties, and her husband can relax, knowing his children are in good hands.

Taurus, Pisces, and Scorpio make good matches. Aries is difficult, once things cool off after the initial honeymoon. When a Capricorn meets another Capricorn, they will be each other's first and last love. Sagittarius isn't a bad match, but they don't always pass the test of time. Aquarius and Capricorn are a difficult match, and rarely found together. Things are too dull with a Virgo, and while Leo can be exciting at first, things will fall apart when he begins showing off. Libra and Aquarius are both difficult partners for Capricorn, and she is rarely found with either of them.

AQUARIUS

A female Aquarius is very different from her male counterparts. She is calm and keeps a cool head, but she is also affectionate and open. She values loyalty above all else, and is unlikely to recover from any infidelity, though she will only divorce if this becomes a chronic trend, and she has truly been stabbed in the back. She is not interested in her partner's money, but rather, his professional success. She is unobtrusive and trusting, and will refrain from listening in on her partner's phone conversations or hacking into his email. With rare exceptions, Aquarian women make terrible housewives. But they are excellent partners in life – they are faithful, never boring, and will not reject a man, even in the most difficult circumstances. Most Aquarians are highly intuitive, and can easily tell the truth from a lie. They themselves only lie in extreme situations, which call for a "white lie" in order to avoid hurting someone's feelings.

Aquarius gets along well with Aries, Gemini, and Libra. She can also have a good relationship with a Sagittarius. Taurus often makes a successful match, though they are emotionally very different; the same goes for Virgo. Aquarius and Scorpio, Capricorn, or Cancer is a difficult match. Pisces can make a good partner as well, as both signs complement each other. Any relationship with a Leo will be tumultuous, but lasting, as Leo is selfish, and Aquarius will therefore have to be very forgiving.

PISCES

Pisces women are very adaptable, musically inclined, and erotic. They possess an innate earthly wisdom, and a good business sense. Pisces often reinvent themselves; they can be emotional, soft, and obstinate, as well as sentimental, at times. Their behavioral changes can be explained by frequent ups and downs. Pisces is charming, caring, and her outward malleability is very attractive to men. She is capable of loving selflessly, as long as the man has something to love. Even if he doesn't, she will try and take care of him until the very end. Pisces' greatest fear is poverty. They are intuitive, vulnerable, and always try to avoid conflict. They love to embellish the truth, and sometimes alcohol helps with this. Rarely, one finds extremely unbalanced, neurotic and dishonest Pisces, who are capable of turning their loved ones' lives into a living Hell!

Taurus, Capricorn, Cancer, and Scorpio make the best matches. She will be greatly attracted to a Virgo, but a lasting relationship is only likely if both partners are highly spiritual. Any union with a Libra is likely to be difficult and full of conflict. Pisces finds Gemini attractive, and they may have a very lively relationship – for a while. Occasionally, Pisces ends up with a Sagittarius, but she will have to fade into the background and entirely submit to him. If she ends up with an Aquarius, expect strong emotional outbursts, and a marriage that revolves around the need to raise their children.

Tatiana Borsch